P9-AFO-284

SPECIAL
HANDLING

Other Books by Mark Pawlak:

Richard Edelman & Mark Pawlak: Poems (West End Chapbook)
The Buffalo Sequence (Copper Canyon)
All The News (Hanging Loose)
Smart Like Me: High-School-Age Writing from the Sixties to Now,
  Co-editor with Dick Lourie (Hanging Loose)

SPECIAL
HANDLING

Newspaper Poems New and Selected

Mark Pawlak

HANGING LOOSE PRESS
BROOKLYN, NEW YORK

Copyright © 1993 by Mark Pawlak

Published by Hanging Loose Press, 231 Wyckoff Street, Brooklyn, New York
11217. All rights reserved. No part of this book may be reproduced with-
out the publisher's written permission, except for brief quotations in reviews.

Printed in the United States of America
10 9 8 7 6 5 4 3 2 1

Hanging Loose Press thanks the Fund For Poetry and the Literature Program
of the New York State Council on the Arts for grants in support of the pub-
lication of this book.

Acknowledgments: Some of these poems first appeared in *5 A.M.*, *Abraxas*,
Blood To Remember: American Poets on the Holocaust, (Texas Tech
University Press), *Exquisite Corpse*, *Five Fingers Review*, *Hanging Loose*,
Hang Together: The Hanging Loose 20th Anniversary Anthology, *Imagine*,
Midwest Alliance, *New Kauri*, *Noctiluca*, *Pig Iron: Third World Issue*,
Polish-American Journal, *Rhino*, *Slipstream*, *Small Pond* and *Transfer*.
"East-West Dialogue, November 1981," "All The News," "Newsbriefs"
and "Atlantic Dispatches" appeared in *All The News*, a Hanging Loose
Press chapbook.

Cover art by Robin Tewes

Library of Congress Cataloging-in-Publication Data

Pawlak, Mark.
    Special handling / Mark Pawlak.
      p. cm.
    ISBN 0-914610-99-6 — ISBN 0-914610-57-0 (paper) :
    I. Title.
    PS3566.A883S67   1993
    811'.54—dc20   93-160
                                                  CIP

Produced at The Print Center., Inc., 225 Varick St.,
New York, NY 10014, a non-profit facility for literary
and arts-related publications. (212) 206-8465

Table of Contents:

Chalatenango

for Mary

SPECIAL HANDLING:

Newspaper Poems New and Selected

VFW BAR TALK

I got one eye.
My feet hangs down.

I got a joint
mashed in my back.

I got a shoulder
been broke —

feel that knot
right there.

But I'd go fight
for my country

today.
You're darn right.

I'd go
right now, boy.

A MERRY BAND

Having an
"obsessive preoccupation
with one or two subjects
that they follow through on
and they don't care
what others think"

defines the eccentric personality,
according to Dr. David Weeks,
principal psychologist at London's
Royal Edinburgh Hospital,
who is conducting a scientific
study of 200 avowed eccentrics.

> A former social worker now lives in a cave
> and takes long walks for charity, barefoot
> and dressed in pajamas. On one occasion,
> he traversed the length of Britain,
> from John o'Groats in the north
> to Land's End at its southern tip...

> A woman with a penchant for pianos
> decided to live on the top floor
> of a building with only narrow
> winding stairs leading to her flat.
> In order to admit her four grand pianos,
> movers had to cut a hole in one wall...

Eccentrics realize they
are different from others,
says Dr. Weeks,
but they think
it is the world that is
out of step with them.

> A man employed by a British firm
> to install bank security devices
> has legally changed his name to Robin Hood
> and goes about the streets of Nottingham
> attired in Lincoln green, carrying a long-
> bow and quiver of arrows...

ALL THE NEWS

ATLANTIC DISPATCHES, 1982

"It does not matter whether the war is actually
happening...it does not matter whether the war is going well or
badly. All that is needed is that a state of war should exist."
— George Orwell, *1984*

April

Raising The Argentine Flag At Port Stanley

The new governor assures the Islanders
that their misgivings are unwarranted:
waking up one morning, for example,
to discover a son or daughter missing —
disappearances, he promises,
will be investigated
as thoroughly as on the mainland.

May

British soldiers boarded ships
bound for the south Atlantic
thinking they had a serious job to do.

Everything they had learned about the last war —
that slaughterhouse their fathers marched into —
they forgot.

In the pubs
their neighbors emptied pints of ale
and spoke of quick and certain victory.

When the first British ship was sunk
they began to sober up.

June

This war was like others before it:
When the fighting ended with the surrender of the
Argentine garrison at Port Stanley a crowd which

gathered at the Presidential palace in Buenos Aires
jeered the Junta for leading the country into defeat.
The urchins of Buenos Aires jeered loud as anyone.

And at the Prime Minister's residence in London another
crowd cheered her for leading the country to victory.
There one of the London urchins led the cheering.

After both crowds had been dispersed
the urchins remained in the streets
hungry and homeless as before the war.

July

Afterword

After the troopships have docked
and after the cheering has subsided

the returning heroes exchange their battle helmets
for the favorite caps they'd left hanging on pegs

then resume their place on street corners
and in the queues outside the employment offices.

ALL THE NEWS, 1983

"They say there is no penalty for poets,
There is no penalty for writing poems.
They say this. This is the penalty."
— Muriel Rukeyser, *In Our Time*

1.

Those who believe what they read in the newspaper
and what they hear reported on the television news
don't want to know the truth.

Those who want to know the truth
don't expect to find it printed in the newspaper
or reported on the television news.

Yet we read the newspaper
and listen to the television news reports.

2.

Those who are in positions of power
say when it comes to free speech
that in *this* country

the newspaper publisher
and the secretary who answers his telephone
are both free to speak their minds.

The thousands who read his newspaper
cannot deny
that the publisher speaks his mind freely.

The women who work in the office beside her
will tell you
his secretary speaks *her* mind freely too.

3.

When the wealthy are less burdened by taxes
they will serve better food at their banquets
and the portions will be larger

and the crumbs that drop from the plates of their guests
which the worker and the unemployed scramble for
will be tastier and more plentiful:

      this is what the President has in mind
      when he says that better times lie ahead.

Old men and women walk the city streets.
They now have paper bags
in which to carry their belongings.

And the welfare mother
has a few slices of bread left on the table this week
to feed her children when they return home from school:

      already the President sees signs
      that things are getting better.

    4.

One day you read in your newspaper
that thousands of people
are demonstrating in the streets of a foreign capital,
protesting their government's policies.
The next day the leader of that nation
arrives at the White House
to confer with the President.
The day after the foreign leader returns home
you find his picture
on the front page of your morning paper —
he is smiling as he steps off the airplane
to greet his loyal ministers —
and you read the report
printed beneath his picture
that small bands of fanatics
are rioting in his streets.

    5.

When the intelligence officer
reads his report in the Senate chamber
that Soviet troops are using chemical weapons in Afghanistan
study the Senators gathered there —
you will find one

rubbing his hands together.
Learn what state he represents and you will know
the location of the Army's new chemical factory.

6. Peacekeeper

"We plan to produce the MX missile, now named 'Peacekeeper,'
and deploy it in superhard silos..."
— President Ronald Reagan

The President says that the more
bombers and missiles the nation builds
the less chance there will be a war.

That's like saying
the more wheat farmers plant
the less grain will be harvested.

If more cattle are herded into stockyards for slaughter
will there be less meat to eat?

When the newest missile is rolled off the assembly line
the President steps to the podium to speak
on the difficulties of waging peace.

In his eyes
every missile is a dove.

NEWSBRIEFS, 1984

"In our time, political speech and writing are largely the
defense of the indefensible... designed to make lies sound
truthful and murder respectable, and to give an appearance
of solidity to pure wind."
      — George Orwell, *Politics and the English Language*

A GUATEMALAN INDUSTRIALIST
SEES SIGNS OF PROGRESS IN HIS COUNTRY

For example:
when peasant girls now fetch water
from springs a few miles beyond their villages
they balance on their heads
jugs made of plastic rather than clay.

*

PROGRESS IS REPORTED IN CONTRACT NEGOTIATIONS
BETWEEN GM AND THE UAW

Because new Chevrolets are collecting snow in factory lots
workers are standing in line outside the unemployment offices
waiting for the doors to open.

It's obvious why the workers are rubbing their hands together:
they are standing outside in the cold.

But why are the officers of the corporation
rubbing *their* hands together?

*

ECONOMIC PICTURE IMPROVING,
SAYS PRESIDENT

Shipyards are hiring again.
Sparks now fly from welders' torches night *and* day.
Warship-building is once more a healthy industry.

*

20

CUTS IN MILITARY SPENDING ANNOUNCED

Generals dining in the Pentagon's cafeterias
now wipe duck sauce from their lips
with paper napkins instead of linen.

*

Lighting the National Christmas Tree

THE PRESIDENT ADMONISHES THOSE AMERICANS
WHO HAVE JOBS
TO REMEMBER THEIR LESS FORTUNATE NEIGHBORS
THIS SEASON OF GIVING

He himself has already presented
needy Guatemala
with a fleet of armored helicopters.

*

A GUATEMALAN BUSINESSMAN
SEES THINGS IN HIS COUNTRY
LOOKING BETTER EVERY DAY

He says when his countrymen look to the future
a smile blossoms on each of their faces:

The Guatemalan businessman looks to the future and smiles.
He has purchased a private airplane
that will seat every member of his family.

The Guatemalan peasant also looks to the future and smiles.
He has acquired a rifle.

WORDS OF WISDOM

"114 year old Augusta Holtz of St. Louis,
Missouri, today revealed her secret for longevity:
'Keep having birthdays!'"
— AP Wire Service

After one Hainan Island boy
nearly died of asphyxiation
with a live fish
stuck in his throat,
the Chinese *Hainan Daily* cautioned:

"With the summer holidays
now here,
teachers
            and parents
must educate children
not to try to catch
fish with their mouths."

*

Asked: "What
do you think about
when you are
in the air?"

Christopher Adams, thirty,
the "human rocket"
who gets shot out of a cannon
in every Ringling Bros.
and Barnum & Bailey Circus show
replied:

"I think about
getting to the net—
reaching
the net."

22

FIRSTS

A Jakarta, Indonesia,
newspaper reported
that Syaiful Bachri, age twenty,

using two rearview
motorcycle mirrors
to watch oncoming traffic,

crossed the island of Java
four hundred ninety-two miles
walking backward.

*

David Berg of LaCrosse, Wisconsin,
performed the feat of folding

himself into a collapsible sofa bed
on "Stupid Human Tricks,"

an occasional feature on the
"Late Night with David Letterman" TV show.

Robert Cerney and Debbie Bermeister
tried to do Berg's feat one better.

Together, naked,
they folded themselves

into the sofa bed in their
Winona, Minnesota, living room.

Berg, on live television,
was able to extricate

himself from the spring loaded trap,
but the Minnesota couple

was only able to free
part of Bermeister's body,

enough for her to reach the telephone
and summon help.

Police Sergeant Dave Gabbert
came to their rescue.

He expressed amazement
that they were able to both fit.

"*I* wouldn't do it,"
Sergeant Gabbert said.

"I guess that's why they call it
'Stupid Human Tricks.'"

*

Syaiful Bachri,
staggering uncontrollably
when he tried to walk normally,

claimed he averaged
eighteen miles a day
during his twenty-eight-day journey.

"Many people along the way
thought I was crazy,"
Bachri said.

"But I'm the first
person to do this
in Indonesia."

MARKS TO BEAT

1.

The annual Watermelon Thump and Seed-Spitting Contest
takes place this June in Luling, Texas,
as it has for the past thirty-five years;
but this year for the first time the town is offering
a one-thousand-dollar grand prize.

Flags emblazoned with watermelons
will line both sides of Luling's Main Street
and eight-foot plastic watermelons
will grace every light pole;
prize watermelons will be auctioned off
and watermelon slices will be served free;
awards will be handed out to persons who eat
the most watermelon in the shortest time
and a Luling High School senior
will be crowned Watermelon Thump Queen;
but the main event, as always,
will be the seed-spitting competition.

Contestants are divided by age into three groups:
seven and under, eight through fourteen,
and the senior division, fifteen and up.
Sixty-five feet four inches is the mark to beat,
the Guiness World Record set in Luling in 1980
by John Wilkinson of Austin.
Only if the record is broken
will the thousand-dollar grand prize be awarded;
otherwise each of the division winners
will get the traditional dollar a foot.

Lem Allen, Jr., a law student
and the 1985 seed-spitting champ
has returned to Luling this year
lured by the big money prize.
He's been practicing, he says,
and has perfected his technique.
"Take a deep breath," Lem Allen explains,
"pick a spot in the air,

and spit," is the way to do it.
"But you've got to be careful
not to breathe in too deep," he warns.
"I've swallowed a couple that way."

Noel "Skip" Allen (no relation)
is another returning seed-spitting champ.
Skip Allen is a two-time winner.
Fifty-three feet six inches is his personal best —
well short of the world record, he admits,
but that won't stop him from trying to better it.
Skip Allen predicts the new grand prize
will bring out a lot of people this year.
He expects the competition to be stiff.
"A thousand bucks," Skip Allen says,
"is a lot of money for spitting seeds."

2.

The 15th annual International Cherry Pit-Spitting Contest
took place on July 2nd in Eau Claire, Wisconsin.
Twelve year old Sara Harris of Berrien Springs
won the youth competition
with a spit of thirty-eight feet eleven inches;
Irene Granbow of East Lansing took the women's division
with a forty-three foot nine inch spit;
and Rick Kraus, thirty-four, of Flint
spat a cherry pit seventy-two feet seven inches
to capture the men's title.
For Kraus, it was an unprecedented
sixth cherry pit-spitting title;
it was also a new world record — more than six feet better
than the mark he set the year before.
"The conditions today were really good,"
Rick Kraus said afterward.
"It wasn't real hot.
The wind was coming out of the northwest,
and it wasn't a strong breeze.
Everything was perfect."

3.

Randy Ober of Bentonville, Arkansas,

spat a wad of tobacco forty-seven feet seven inches,
on April 4th, 1982,
at the 5th annual Calico
Tobacco Chewing and Spitting Championships,
north of Barstow, California.
His mark set a world record,
which remains unsurpassed.

DIFFERENT BUT SIMILAR

EAST-WEST DIALOGUES

"Then came the barbarians. They too highly valued the little
god of irony. They would crush it under their heels and add
it to their dishes."

— Zbigniew Herbert, "From Mythology"

November 1981

Polish Worker and American Worker

In my country
the workers have money to spend
because in the stores
the shelves are empty.

> In my country
> the shelves are crowded with goods
> few workers can afford to buy.

In my country the workers must stand in line
outside the bakery for hours in the cold
waiting for the doors to open
to buy a loaf of bread.

> In my country the workers also
> stand in line for hours in the cold
> waiting for the doors to open.

Outside the bakery?

> Outside the unemployment office.

When the workers in my country complain
government officials only speak louder
to drown their voices out.

> It's the same in my country.

When the workers strike
the newspapers in my country
call the leaders subversives.

It's the same in my country.

Do your newspapers report our workers' demand
for a voice in managing the factories?

      Yes. They speak of the Polish workers'
      heroic struggle for democracy.

Do American workers make similar demands?

      Yes.

And what do your newspapers say?

      That they are Communist-inspired.

*

June 1990

Senate Majority Leader George Mitchell and
Soviet President Mikhail S. Gorbachev:

People in the Baltic Republic of Lithuania
complain they are under the yoke of Soviet rule.
They say the Soviet troops now in Vilnius
are invaders, an occupation army. They wish to be free.

> The same thing can be said about American troops in Panama.
> Didn't your armed forces invade that independent nation?
> Your soldiers are now quartered in the capital there.
> Aren't they also an occupation army? Why the double standard?

No. It is different. People in the streets of Panama City
cheered the American soldiers, even as the fighting still raged;
welcomed them as their liberators from the tyrant Noriega.
So Panamanians were quoted as saying in newspaper accounts.
So they spoke before television cameras,
while standing amid the rubble of their own houses.

> I can assure you, Senator, that in 1979 our Moscow
> newspaper and television reports from Afghanistan
> also showed people in the streets of Kabul
> cheering our Soviet troops.

*

January 1991

American Worker and Polish Worker

Polish workers used to joke
about how they had money in their pockets
because in the stores
the shelves were always empty.

> That was in the old days,
> under Communism with central planning;
> but since our 1989 revolution
> things have changed for the better.

Since '89, the newspapers here in my country
speak of the 'new' Poland.

> Yes, we have democracy and free enterprise now,
> just as you do in America.

Our president and our leaders in Congress
now hail your country
as the "pioneer of capitalism" in Eastern Europe.

> In Poland, just as in America,
> the shelves are now fully stocked
> with consumer goods imported from the West:
> blue jeans, French perfumes, pornographic videos...
> you name it!

Just as here in America...

> Warsaw even has a Mercedes showroom,
> a Christian Dior boutique...

Do you mean that Polish workers now wear
high-fashion clothes and drive Mercedes?

> No. Not at all...
> not many of us can afford the items
> we see on display now in store windows.

Ah, of course,
just as here in America.
And those few who can...?

>The few who can are mostly
>former top government officials,
>now in the private sector.

Of course,
just as here in America.

ADS AND TRADING CARDS

Electroliers

The search for motif;
the choice of pleasing lines;
a base in harmony with the hand decorated shade;
the fashioning from durable materials...
in the making of these electric lamps
every device of the artist-craftsman
is brought into full play.
        — Ad for lamps, "Country Life in America," 1906

*

    Roman

All the imperial desire for imperishable beauty
found in Roman architecture and decoration
show forth in this Electric Lamp.

*

    Viking

Noted in this lamp
are the bold,
venturesome characteristics
of these Sea Rovers;

with its shade
of rich, barbaric colors,
adorned with prow-like
heads of sea monsters.

*

    Italian Renaissance

A notable work of art,
gorgeous, stately,
flushed with the colors
of grape
and sun
and sky.

*

36

Louis XIV

A royal lamp —
massive and ornate,
as was the style of the Period,
but always balanced,
and executed with fine dignity.

*

Louis XV

Fit to have adorned the rich table
of the Divine Monarch.

Lightheartedness and gaiety
characterized his reign;

and lightheartedness and gaiety
are expressed in this lamp's

delicate tracery of line and curve,
combined with an ornate exuberance.

*

Colonial

Restrained in curve and line
to harmonize precisely
with the Colonial design.

The colors are subdued
and have a chastened effect.
Tall and graceful,

it still typifies
the severe dignity
which distinguishes the Puritan.

"Indian Life in the '60s" Trading Cards
c. 1910

for Sherman Alexie and Ron Overton

1. *Race of Young Bucks:*

   The foot race
   has always been a sport
   very much practiced
   and enjoyed by the Indians,
   who were very fleet of foot.

   Some of the swiftest
   and best known
   amateur runners of today
   are full-blooded Indians.

2. *Peace Offering to the Spirit of the Dead Bear:*

   The Indians had a superstitious dread
   of killing a grizzly bear
   as they thought it would bring them
   bad luck.

   Sometimes a bear would be killed
   when food could be obtained no other way,
   or in self-protection.

   The Indian would then endeavor to appease
   the offended spirit of the dead bear
   by offering him the peace pipe.

   This picture illustrates such an incident.

3. *Squaw Gathering Grapes:*

   The Indians tilled the soil but very little
   and depended for food on the vegetables,
   roots and fruits that grew wild.

   Here an Indian squaw is shown
   gathering wild grapes
   to be dried and used in winter.

Her papoose or baby she has taken with her
and is seen wrapped up in the Indian fashion,
hanging on the branch of a convenient tree.

4. *Indian Children Crying:*

There is a popular belief
that the Indian papooses
never cry:

this is not so.

It is true
that they are
more stoical than white children,
inheriting these qualities
from their savage parents.

Here a papoose
and an older brother are wailing
because of their being left alone,
apparently deserted.

5. *Indian Lover Serenading His Sweetheart:*

Indians do not as a rule
suggest to our mind anything
in connection with love of sentiment,
                              yet

their young men and young women
were no different
from others in this respect.

The flute was thought by them
to have a peculiar charm
for the Indian maiden

and its notes
could always be heard
at night around an Indian village.

"Movie of a Day with Towle's Log Cabin Syrup"

— "Ladies Home Journal" ad, 1917

Panel 1:
"The children have Log Cabin on their cereal."

Panel 2:
"Father has Log Cabin on his waffles."

Panel 3:
"Log Cabin makes the grapefruit delicious."

Panel 4:
"Father's lunch consists of Log Cabin, griddle cakes and milk."

Panel 5:
"Jane's maple cake owes its rich flavor to Log Cabin."

Intermission:
"The Sweet-of-a-Hundred-Uses
in the famous Log-Cabin-shaped can
means purity, healthfulness, wholesomeness
for all the family."

Panel 6:
"The children love Log Cabin and bread after school."

Panel 7:
"Log Cabin makes wonderful maple fudge."

Panel 8:
"Mother's famous maple cookies are flavored with Log Cabin."

Panel 9:
"A delicious Sundae — ice cream and Log Cabin."

Credits:
"Granulated Sugar, Maple Sugar."

Dress Well and Succeed

— Ad for Paris Garters, c. 1928

Not once
but many times
she noticed his socks

Could he have
read her thoughts
he would not
have lost her

(Dress Well
and Succeed).

A picture of neatness
herself
she detested
slovenliness

(Paris Garters
Dress Well and Succeed).

His ungartered socks
crumpling down
around his shoe tops
—and he wonders why she said "NO!"

(Paris Garters
No Metal Can Touch You

Single Grip
or Double Grip

Dress Well and Succeed.)

SIMILAR BUT DIFFERENT

Trish McDonald and Frances Miller
both live in California,
but in different cities,
but both live in cities bearing saints' names —
Trish McDonald in San Jose,
Frances Miller in Santa Clara;
and both are married — but Trish McDonald
only very recently, while Frances Miller
has been married for many years.
And they both recently experienced
the loss of a treasured possession.

Trish McDonald, on the eve of her wedding,
accidentally flushed her engagement ring down the toilet.
Frances Miller had a religious relic stolen —
not just any relic,
but her Vatican authenticated St. Jude relic.
Frances Miller is devoted to St. Jude,
who was one of Christ's original twelve apostles.
"I couldn't have been more upset," she said,
"if someone stole my husband."
Trish McDonald was just as upset about her ring. She said,
"I just about hyperventilated on the floor."

But whereas Trish McDonald's
diamond studded, gold engagement ring
was valued at over five thousand dollars,
Frances Miller's St. Jude relic
was only "worth very, very little" monetarily;
however, the two thousand-year-old bone fragment,
which was smaller in size than a silver dollar
and set in a glass container at the center
of a five-inch-long gold-plated cross,
was to its owner "beyond value" spiritually.

Trish McDonald and Frances Miller...two California women.
Each lost an object which she cherished,
but one was inadvertently responsible for her loss;
while the other had the loss inflicted upon her.

The day before her wedding,
Trish McDonald, who is a flight attendant,
got up from bed and went to wash her face, as usual.
But first she took her ring off
and wrapped it in toilet paper to protect it. Afterward,
she had wiped the sink dry with some other toilet paper.
She then collected it all together, and without thinking,
flushed the whole bunch down the toilet.

Frances Miller, a housewife, got the bad news one day
in a phone call from her parish priest. He informed her
that Our Lady of Peace Church had been broken into,
and that her St. Jude relic,
which had been on display there on loan for weeks,
was now missing.

"This is the beginning of the end of my marriage,"
Trish McDonald said she thought to herself
when she realized what she had done.
Frances Miller in contrast just felt burning mad.
She hoped the thieves were Catholic, she said,
so that, in addition to going to jail (if caught),
they could also be excommunicated.

     II

Dean Williamson in the San Jose Roto-Rooter office
took the call from Trish McDonald about her ring.
"It was a real long shot," he said.
"I didn't think myself that we'd ever get it."
Williamson nevertheless set to work, assisted by his crew
made up of Robert Rutz, Jerry Supernaw and Richard Burton.

First the men examined Trish McDonald's toilet
with mirrors and probes. The ring wasn't there.
Next they tore up the lawn in front of the house
to check the sewer pipes leading to the street.
It wasn't there either. As a last try,
they constructed a special dam inside the sewer main
that runs beneath Paseo Estero Drive outside Trish McDonald's house,
and, using their big Hydro-Flush unit truck,
flooded the thirty-six-inch diameter pipe

with hundreds of gallons of water. That did the trick.
The ring was caught in the dam and retrieved.

Trish McDonald screamed out loud
and jumped up and down for joy
when the Roto-Rooter team reported their success.
She was exceedingly grateful, too.
Trish McDonald said she gave the men
"all the champagne out of my refrigerator."

Officers of the Santa Clara Police Department
meanwhile had told Frances Miller
the chances were at best very slim
that her St. Jude relic would ever turn up.
And the reward she is offering for its return —
one hundred dollars, no questions asked —
has so far not enticed the thieves to give it back.
Nevertheless Frances Miller remains hopeful.
Frances Miller may have lost her relic,
but she never lost her faith.
She is counting, she says, on the power of prayer;
the daily petitions for help she makes to St. Jude:
Jude, the patron saint of impossible causes.

WIRE SERVICE

"You should always believe all you read
in the newspapers, as this makes them more interesting."
— Dame Rose Macauley

MOTIVATION

One hundred twenty hours fifteen minutes,
the marathon record for typewriting on a manual machine,
held by Mike Howell of Liverpool, England,
a blind office worker, has now been surpassed
by Shamboo Anbhawane of Bombay, India,
a forty-four-year-old professional typist.

Two different entries for pogo stick jumping are included
in the 1988 edition of the Guinness Book of World Records,
both marks held by Ashrita Furman of New York City:
the distance record, eleven and three-tenths miles,
which he set by hopping up and back down Mt. Fuji in Japan,
and the record for underwater pogoing, three hours forty minutes,
which he established beneath the Amazon River in Peru.

And two Canadian men,
Peter DiBernardi, forty-two, of Niagara Falls, Ontario,
and Jeffrey Petkovich, twenty-five, of Ottawa,
have become the eighth and ninth persons to survive
a trip over Niagara Falls in a barrel;
but they will go down in record books for being the
first *pair* ever to do so in the same barrel.

*

Shamboo Anbhawane repeatedly typed an eight-page speech
by the chairman of Hindustan Lever of India, Ltd.
He started at noon on a Monday, typing sixty words per minute,
and finished after three p.m. the following Saturday,
eight hundred thousand keystrokes later, typing only fifteen.
Anbhawane's hands and arms shook violently
after his long days and sleepless nights of continuous typing.
"I can't speak, I can't speak," he told reporters
when they asked him what he thought about his achievement.
"It is beyond words!"

Ashrita Furman recently broke his own 1988 pogo distance mark.
First he circled a quarter-mile racing track in New York City
forty times for a total of ten miles.
He then bounced up Third Avenue, three more miles,

to the foot of the Empire State Building,
wearing out two specially designed
heavy duty pogo sticks during the day.
Furman, a desciple of Sri Chinmoy,
dedicated his latest pogo hopping feat to his guru.
"I used to be a totally unathletic nerd," he said,
"but then I got involved in meditation."

Peter DiBernardi and Jeffrey Petkovich
put their specially constructed "barrel"
into the swift flowing Niagara River above the Horseshoe Falls,
navigated the upper rapids to the brink,
plummeted one hundred seventy-six feet, and then negotiated
treacherous whirlpools and rapids in the gorge below.
Three others who had previously attempted the same trip
did not survive, according to Constable David Jahns
of the Niagara Parks Police; but, he said,
DiBernardi and Petkovich emerged from their ten-foot long,
four-foot diameter, foam-lined metal cylinder
with only "very, very minor cuts and scrapes."

*

Shamboo Anbhawane kept Indian devotional music playing
in the background during the entire one hundred
twenty-three hours that he sat hunched over his machine.
"Whenever I found it monotonous," he said,
"I typed Lord Rama's name."

Ashrita Furman could have, would have gone even further,
hopping up the steps to the top of the Empire State Building,
but managers of the hundred-and-two-story-high landmark
refused him permission. Setting the new record,
Furman explained, was a present to himself
in celebration of his thirty-fifth birthday.

Peter DiBernardi and Jeffrey Petkovich
said they hoped that their death-defying plunge
over the falls in a barrel
would make a statement about drugs
to young people throughout the world.

Police Constable Jahns expressed sympathy with their motive,
but was nevertheless compelled by duty to impound their "barrel"
and bring the two men before a magistrate for arraignment
on charges of "performing an unlawful stunt on Niagara Park grounds."

DiBernardi and Petkovich said in their own defense:
"We just wanted to show kids
there's a lot better things for them to do
than be on the brink of dope."

THREE HEADLINES, 1986

1. SOUTH KOREA COMPLAINS OF "MISLEADING TERMS"
   USED BY THE FOREIGN PRESS IN REPORTING RECENT
   DEVELOPMENTS

    Reporters describing
    the confinement
    of dissident politicians
    to their homes
    by police troops
    are asked to stop using
    the inaccurate term
    "house arrest," as no
    warrants for arrest
    have been issued.

    The Seoul government
    suggests that reporters
    use in its place
    the more exact term
    "preventive restraint."

*

2. A SALVADORAN COFFEE PLANTER SEES RECENT GOVERN-
   MENT REFORMS AS NOTHING BUT GIVEAWAYS

    He says they give away everything to the peasants
    while plantation owners like himself
    get only headaches.

    The *campesinos* he hires to pick his coffee beans
    have had their wages raised by government decree.
    At the same time, the rent he collects from them
    has been lowered. Next thing, he expects
    that during peak harvest he will have to allow
    one day off to rest out of every seven.
    Headaches! Headaches! Now, each morning,
    the planter instructs his housekeeper
    to bring the aspirin bottle to his bedside
    along with the newspaper. And he waits

until he feels the medicine take effect
before reading the latest official decree,
which, he says, only informs him
how much poorer he has become overnight.

*

3. CAMBODIAN GUERRILLA SPONSORSHIP DRIVE
   ANNOUNCED

The Khmer People's National Liberation Front,
one of three insurgent armies
fighting Vietnamese troops in Cambodia,
has today opened its "Sponsor a Guerrilla" drive
from offices in New York City.

In newspaper ads, as well as a glossy brochure,
Americans sympathetic to the Cambodian cause
of freedom from the hated Vietnamese invaders
are invited to sponsor a guerrilla fighter.

A donation of only $40, the ads and brochure explain,
will buy: 2 uniforms
           2 sets of underwear
           1 pair of shoes
           1 pair of socks
           1 knapsack
           1 hammock
           1 plastic sheet,
           and 1 traditional Khmer scarf, or *krama*
           (which can double as loincloth or turban).

Compounding the satisfaction donors can take
in helping a cause they view as good
will be a gift of the sponsored guerrilla's
photograph, wallet size;
also the promise of letters from the front,
as battlefield conditions allow.

SIGNS OF PROGRESS IN THE '80s

1983:
TURKISH PHARMACEUTICALS MAGNATE
SEES A SUNNY FUTURE FOR HIS COUNTRY
— *Atlantic Monthly*

Since the martial law of the Colonels
has restored order
no longer does Nejat Eczacibasi
travel in an armored limousine
to oversee
production at his factories
but instead
now drives his own
vintage Stutz (1932)
Super Bearcat convertible
with the top down.

*

1984:
PROGRESS IN HONDURAS

In outlying hamlets
where doctors had been unknown
the stooped peasants
lugging sacks of corn

now ease their backaches
with aspirin at bedtime
thanks to U.S. medics.

                *

And at Puerto Lempira
before the Army Corps of Engineers arrived
only an occasional light plane
would put down at this dirt airstrip

now heavy transports
land every day on a concrete runway
extending a thousand yards into the jungle

and women from the nearby villages
who used to stare at their toes
when a foreigner spoke to them

now gather outside the barracks compound
and call through the fence
to Yankee soldiers they seem to know by name.

                *

And close to the border with Nicaragua
the Indian who used to walk dirt footpaths
or roads that were two ruts through trees
hunting with bow & arrow

now rides in the back of a truck
on recently graded tarmac roads
oiling an M-16 rifle.

*

1985:
CONSTITUTIONAL REFERENDUM IN HAITI TODAY
— 22 July, New York *Times*

The last time Haitians went
to the polls 14 years ago,
the 19-year-old Jean-Claude
"Baby Doc" Duvalier
was confirmed as the country's
President-for-Life,
succeeding his father
"Papa Doc" in that post.

The vote tally according to official
government figures from the time
was 2,391,916
in favor
and none against.

Today's referendum will
provide for a Prime Minister
to serve
at "the pleasure" of Mr. Duvalier;
a step which the U.S.
State Department is hailing
as "progress toward democracy."
Overwhelming voter approval
is expected.

1987:
CONDITIONS FOR SOUTH AFRICAN BLACKS ARE SEEN
TO IMPROVE

On Weiler's Farm, twenty miles outside Johannesburg,
illegal black squatters,
subject to arrest under the Pass Law,
used to make their homes
inside the abandoned stables and pigsties
to avoid the eyes of police inspectors.

But now, since the Pass Law has been abolished,
they've come out into the open.
Their new-made shacks, constructed of cardboard,
scrap tin, and lumber saved from packing crates,
stand on Weiler's Farm now in clusters
all around those same pigsties and stables.

*

1988:
HUMAN RIGHTS VIOLATIONS DECREASE SHARPLY
IN EL SALVADOR

Salvadoran Army joke — question:

Why is it better to cover a corpse with dirt
in a shallow hole in the ground,
than leave it to rot exposed at the roadside?

*

Salvadoran academics' joke:

Those who teach in U.S. colleges and universities
say that it's publish or perish.
But for professors here in El Salvador,
it's publish *and* perish.

*

Salvadoran Army joke — answer:

Because then the corpse is less likely
to attract foreign journalists
and other kinds of vultures.

*

CODA: 1989
"THE PROSPECT FOR LASTING PEACE" IS TOPIC OF BUSH'S
RADIO BROADCAST TO NATION
— after Bertolt Brecht's *Die Kriegsfibel*

When the President speaks of lasting peace over the radio,
the waitress in the diner, pausing to listen,
rests her piping hot orders on the counter.

The President speaks of lasting peace
and the farmer listens intently, eating lunch in his car
parked at the edge of the half-plowed field.

The logger stops sawing
to turn up the volume on his portable radio
when he hears the President speak of lasting peace.

The construction worker, the foundry worker, the aircraft worker
also have their radios tuned to the President's broadcast.

One looks at the superhighway concrete
poured knee-deep to carry heavy tanks;

one runs his big, scarred hand
the length of the Howitzer barrel;

one studies the new "Stealth" B-2 bomber
as it is rolled out through the hangar doors —

all three of them giving serious consideration
to these harbingers.

1990
AS THE ECONOMY WORSENS, CUTBACKS IN HIGHER
EDUCATION HAVE REACHED THE IVY LEAGUE
— National Public Radio news

Traditional cloth
placemats on tables
have been done away with
in dining halls at Smith College,
while at Vassar
paper napkins
have replaced linen.

AIRSTREAMERS

"...say or print nothing
that may reflect unfavorably on others;
maintain our camps in an orderly manner
and leave them in the same way."
— from The Wally Byam Creed

Wally Byam unveiled his first Airstream travel trailer
with its torpedo-shaped, riveted aluminum shell
in January 1936, more than fifty years ago.
A successful Los Angeles businessman
born on the Fourth of July,
he became the pied piper of travel caravaning.

"Traveling by trailer
is in my opinion the best way
to see the world —
or any part of it," he once wrote.
"Of course, I'm prejudiced,
I manufacture travel trailers."

The Wally Byam Club today boasts a membership
of eighteen thousand, mostly retired people.
Club members in their Airstream trailers
band together each year for the annual
international rally and convention, which
finishes on July 4th, for symbolic reasons.

This year, as is traditional, the rally opened
with a prayer offered by club chaplain Dan Wilson:
"Our Heavenly Father, the wheels have spun,
the trailers have rolled through rain, and we're here;
so, Lord, make us happy,
as happy as we can be."

*

Meticulously arranged caravan camps
with the trailers parked in geometric patterns
are a club trademark. This year

three thousand nine hundred sixty-five trailers
converged on Lake Placid, New York,
for the 28th International Grand Rally

and assumed rally formation
on a one hundred forty acre plot
with knife-edge precision.

Seen from two miles away,
the valley below the Lake Placid Olympic ski jump
appeared flooded by a sea of mercury.

Up close, it looked more like a
small city had rolled into town
virtually overnight.

The club's long-distance caravan coordinator,
Jack Reifschneider, explained why Airstreamers
arrange themselves so neatly.

"We're kind of orderly people," he said.
"We're proud of our trailers,
and we're proud of our club.

"We don't want communities to think
we're a bunch of bums coming through.
We weren't before we retired, you know."

*

Precision is also everything
for sixty-nine-year-old Daisy Mae Dearth,
who for thirteen years has directed
the Wally Byam usherettes.

Mrs. Dearth was the first woman
to usher at a major convention.
Soon the men asked her to take over.
"I said there are a few stipulations:

"I can pick them myself;
I can dress them alike,
and I can call them usherettes."
Each year she utilizes thirty usherettes.

It is always a secret
what they will be wearing.
"Everyone is anxious the first day
to see what we have on."

This year they are dressed in red,
white and blue, with big bows
that look like butterflies. Butterflies
are a rally theme this year.

And they always wear white gloves,
an usherette trademark.
"If their gloves aren't clean,
I'll send them back to their trailers."

Mrs. Dearth says that
her thirty years as an electrician
at a Pensacola, Florida, Navy base
taught her how to boss people around.

*

When the Wally Byam Trailer Club band
struck up "Stars and Stripes Forever,"
the nine thousand members in attendance
at the 28th annual Wally Byam
International Trailer Club Convention
rose in their seats — the traditional
parade of flags had started. Presidents
of one hundred seventy-three chapters
carrying their trailer-unit flags
marched solemnly down the center aisle
of the Lake Placid, New York, Olympic Arena.
If someone called to them, they marched
right by just like guards
at the Tomb of the Unknown Soldier, not
acknowledging anything.
"Sure I was nervous," Ohio chapter president
Dorothy Reigle, said later.
"The first time I saw the flag ceremony
back in '73, I cried. Who wouldn't?"

II

Wally Byam Club members have
no religious slant or philosophy.
"The only cause might be
if some injustice was being done
to recreational vehicles,"
said club spokesman Lou van Dyck.

They hate when people say they are snobby.
"Tent campers seem to think Airstreamers,
like the Cabots and Lodges,
speak only to God," van Dyck said,
"so we work hard
speaking to everyone."

And they hate for people to call them Byamites.
Said one twenty-seven-year club member,
"We're not a cult or anything."

*

"Even our best friends and our family
don't understand our way of life,"
admitted Gay Trowbridge, a retired
Kingston, New York, insurance executive.

She and her husband Bernard, both in their 50s,
have been full-time Airstreamers
since the day three years ago
when Bernard retired from IBM.

They say the adjustment
from house to trailer has been hardest
on their three grown daughters.
"There were lots of tears," Gay recalled.

"They don't understand why we gave up
our beautiful fourteen-room house
that we'd just had redone,
and then bought a trailer and took off.

"One of our daughters said. 'You
weren't supposed to leave home.
We were.'
We're trying to educate them."

*

"I bequeath this creed..."
Wally Byam wrote before his death,
"to lead caravans
wherever the four winds blow...

"over twinkling boulevards,
across trackless deserts...
to the traveled and untraveled
corners of the earth."

In 1955 Wally Byam led a caravan
of five hundred trailers to Mexico. The next year
he led a thirty-six-trailer cavalcade
on a tour through sixteen European countries.

Then in 1959, he headed a charge
of forty-one trailers the length of Africa
from Capetown to Cairo,
a nine-thousand-mile trek.

And when he died, in 1962,
he was planning the legendary
Round-the-World Caravan,
Singapore to Lisbon,

"...a mechanized caravan
threading the trail
spice-bearing camels
once trod..."

*

"Man has within him a desire
to venture forth and be nomadic,"
claims Frank Sargent. "It's only
for the last five hundred generations,

a wink of an eye historically,
that men have been settling down in one place."
The 75-year-old businessman, fellow club members say,
is made of the same stuff as Wally Byam.
Frank Sargent created a revolution in the 50s
when he invented the Port-A-Potti.
Now he is organizing a caravan of eleven
couples from the club to travel through China,
which previously had been closed to trailers.

It took Mr. Sargent a year and a half
to get permission from China. Negotiations stalled
when tourist officials wanted the Americans
to take a Chinese driving test.
"Their Mr. Big was adamant," Sargent recalls. "I said,
'I can't tell my people to take a test.
I will lose face.' That stopped him.
I read about 'face' in China."
Sargent insisted that an International License should do.
"Finally Mr. Big asked, 'Will you
study our rules?'" It was agreed.
Frank Sargent says, "The Chinese
are going to be amazed.
They've never seen anything like us."

AIRSTREAMERS is drawn from the following sources:
"Through Europe by Trailer Caravan," Norma Miller, *National Geographic,* June 1957, Vol. CXI, No. 6.
"Wally Byam — The Man and The Myth," Charles Kiefer, *Trailer Life,* March 1981.
"Trailer Buffs Assemble A Village of Fellowship," Michael Winerip, *New York Times,* July 1, 1985.
"To Airstreamers, a Nomad's Life is the Good Life," Doug Stewart, *Smithsonian,* December 1985.

GERMAN LESSONS

"Anyone who closes his eyes to the past is blind
to the present. Whoever refuses to remember the
inhumanity is prone to new risks of infection."
— West German President
Richard von Weizsacker, 1985

TREBLINKA

German Lesson: *Die Verarbeitung,* Processing

> "All that matters now is Treblinka.
> It is our destiny."
> — sung by the Jewish work crew.

In the words of SS *Unterscharführer,* Franz Suchomel, Treblinka was a "primitive but efficient production line of death." Operating at full capacity, the camp would receive three, sometimes four trains daily; thirty to fifty cars in each, he explains. Of the three, four, five thousand Jews packed into the cars like sardines, upon arrival, as many as a third might already be dead (because of the overcrowding and lack of food and water, or because, in despair, they had slit their wrists or taken poison). These corpses were stacked, neatly as cordwood, by the thousand on the unloading ramp at Treblinka. As for the living: The old and feeble were separated out first, and led or carried away on stretchers to an area called the "infirmary," where a white flag painted with a red cross flew overhead. There they were "cured with a single pill," as the guards joked — a bullet in the neck; and their bodies thrown into a pit. The healthy were separated, men to the right, women to the left side of the ramp, and made to strip; their clothing collected and saved for later use by the German army. Naked, they were then driven by shouting guards wielding leather whips — *Schnell! Schnell!* — through a passage lined with barbed wire called the *Himmelweg* or "Road to Heaven" (by the guards), uphill to the open bunker doors of the gas chamber; men first, followed by the women and children. The entire operation, from arrival at Treblinka station until death, required less than three hours per trainload. This, says *Unterscharführer* Suchomel, was the routine. This was how Jews were "processed" (in German, *verarbeitet*) each day at Treblinka , between 12,000 and 15,000 of them — and *not*, he emphasizes, *not* the 18,000 figure cited by some Jews today.

AUSCHWITZ

Unforgettable

> "The struggle of man against power is the
> struggle of memory against forgetting."
> — Milan Kundera

A man who, in his youth in Poland,
was once publicly whipped, receiving thirty lashes
for refusing to salute a Nazi soldier,
tells of the dogs used by SS guards
to terrorize Jews at Auschwitz:
German shepherds that would, on command,
bite and tear the buttocks
of anyone wearing the prisoner's striped uniform.

Some of these dogs were specially trained,
at a signal, to grab a man by the collar
and drag him to the ground.
Given a second signal, the dog
would pin the man down
with its muzzle to his throat;
and, given a third signal,
bite.

Forty years later, he cannot forget
how the guards made a sport
of setting these trained dogs on prisoners;
he cannot forget the third signal.

Unforgettable II

Another man,
called a "bearer of secrets" by his Nazi jailers
because of what he'd witnessed
as a slave laborer in their death camps,
says that he has forgotten
not one detail of the Auschwitz "undressing room,"
where his assigned task had been
to gather up the discarded clothing.

As he now tells it,
the real purpose of the "undressing room"
was to keep hidden from Jews the truth of their destiny.
Made to resemble rooms travelers of that day could find
in International Information Centers at border crossings,
the victims would pass through it
on their way to the gas chamber,
thinking they were to be de-loused.

On the walls hung hooks for clothing,
each hook with a number;
and beneath these stood wooden benches —
so that people might undress
"more comfortably," the SS guards said.

To complete the resemblance, signs
with slogans printed in several languages
were posted on the pillars that supported the roof.
"Wash Yourself!" they read,
"Clean is Good!" "Lice can Kill!" ...
in several different languages.

And mounted on the walls were other printed signs;
these, in the shapes of arrows, pointed the way
"To the Disinfection Area."

He demonstrates the way Nazi guards
would bow to the Jews standing naked in the room,
deeply from the waist in mock formality;
then, speaking with mock politeness
while gesturing with one hand, they would say:
"This way, please, Ladies, Gentlemen...."

These things he once saw, he says, he can never forget.

First, Undress

> "It is the camp law: people going to their
> deaths must be deceived to the very end."
> — Tadeusz Borowski

One morning at about 4 a.m., while the rest of the Lager slept, Filip Müller, a Jew from Prague, was rousted from his bunk in Cell 13, Block 11, Auschwitz 1 by SS guards and ordered to stand in readiness with the other men in his work detail. Twenty years old and in good health when he arrived at Auschwitz, Müller had been selected for a labor gang instead of being sent directly to the gas chamber. He was assigned to work in the crematorium as a member of the *Sonderkommando,* or "special" detail.

This particular morning, as Müller now tells the story, it was still dark when his detail was led into the yard outside the crematorium where several hundred Jews, newly arrived by transport, had been herded by SS guards. There, under spotlights, while Müller's detail stood by, an SS officer, Aumeyer —he hasn't forgotten the name—addressed the victims. They were Jews from the Sosnowitz ghetto in Upper Silesia, elderly people, mostly, and women with children; their transport papers stamped in German "SB", *Sonderbehandlung,* that is, designated for "special handling." Müller says he watched in silence, forbidden under threat of death from speaking to any to give them warning; but says that he was standing close enough to hear them whispering and caught a few Yiddish words. He heard: *fachowitz,* meaning "skilled worker;" *Malach-ha-Mawis,* "the Angel of Death;" *Harginnen,* "They're going to kill us"...

The SS man, Aumeyer, spoke. "You have nothing to fear," he said. "You're here to work for our soldiers at the front. Those who can work will be all right."

Uncertain of their fate, the assembled Jews listened attentively; some could be seen who were still clutching bundles.

Aumeyer continued: "We need masons, electricians, all the trades." Then he paused a moment, surveying the crowd to judge the effect of his words.

He pointed to a man and asked, "You, what is your trade?"

The man replied, "A tailor."

"A tailor? What kind of tailor?"

"A man's ...No, for both men and women."

"Wonderful!" Aumeyer exclaimed."We need people like you in our workshops."

Then he questioned a woman: "What is your trade?"

And the woman answered, "A nurse."

"Splendid! We need nurses for our wounded soldiers in the hospitals." And to the congregation: "We need you all," he added. "But first, undress. You must be disinfected. We need you healthy."

The Jews began to remove their clothing. As they did, Aumeyer turned and faced the SS men. Müller could see that Aumeyer was beaming with pride at his success.

Speaking to his subordinates: "You see?" Aumeyer said. "You see? That's the way to do it!"

Like Butterflies

after Charles Reznikoff; for Donna Brook

The Auschwitz "Angel of Death," Josef Mengele,
would meet the trains delivering Jews to the camp
and select out from those destined for the gas
healthy pairs of twins. These he kept alive
in crowded cages for genetic experiments
to aid him in building a master race.

He gave them chemical injections
which made many nauseous and faint, and a few
became numb when the needles were put into their spines.
Some were given transfusions of blood
from one twin to the other,
or he removed parts of the sexual organs;
yet others he sterilized by radiation.

He was especially interested in the colors of eyes.
If he noticed that twins' eyes were brown
but their mother's eyes were blue,
he might keep her alive in the cage with her children.
He would try to change their eye color
with injections of dye or with drops administered daily
that burned the eyes like acid,
and he would take blood samples from these subjects
several times each day.

One twin said she was stupefied
when ushered into Mengele's private laboratory.
There she saw an entire wall of eyes looking back at her,
human eyes of every color
mounted on the wall like butterflies.

CHALATENANGO (1980)

"The subversives like to say that they are the fish and the
people are the ocean. What we have done in the north is to
dry up the ocean so we can catch the fish easily."
— A Salvadoran Army commander,
Boston Globe 1980

"they don't speak to the imagination
there are too many of them
the numeral zero at the end
changes them into an abstraction"
— Zbigniew Herbert, "Mr. Cogito
Reads the Newspaper"

Prologue:
Abuelito, **Little Grandfather**

Among one band of Salvadoran peasants who sought refuge
across the border at a Red Cross camp in Honduras
was a seven-year-old orphan boy.
Asked when he had last eaten meat,
the boy replied that he'd forgotten the taste of it;
his family couldn't afford meat.

The boy explained that only rarely
did they get fruits or vegetables,
that his parents had fed him tortillas with beans,
and if there were no beans, as was frequently the case,
then just tortillas. He added
that after the *Guardia Nacional* murdered his parents,
and while he was hiding in the mountains —
he couldn't say for how long, perhaps a month —
he'd often gone hungry. Begging food,
he had got plain, dry tortillas to eat cold —
and those, he said, usually stale.

Abuelito, little grandfather, the boy was nicknamed:
his hair, once jet-black, now from his meager diet
as white as an old man's.

1. *Campesinos*

They are the "have-nots" —
peasants, poor and uneducated.
There are many things
they know nothing about,
but these things they do know:
We own nothing,
not the houses we live in,
not the land they are built upon... .
We are always hungry...
and ... *our children*
cannot go to school
because they have no clothes to wear.

If they should get sick, they explain,
We cannot afford aspirin,
let alone money to see a doctor.
Jobs are impossible to find...
unless it is the harvest season;
then, we work from dawn to dusk
for 2 'colones' a day —
not enough the pay the rent
on one hectare of land.

What can they do?
If we speak up,
we get called 'subversives'.
One complained that he should be paid more
and the hacienda foreman accused him
of speaking against the government.
His body was found in a ditch the next morning.
His tongue had been cut out with a machete
and his head stuck on a pole beside the road
where no peasant could miss seeing it.

2. ORDEN: *Organización Democrática Nacionalista*

"You don't choose to join ORDEN, they choose you
...to refuse would brand you as a 'subversive'."
— a former ORDEN member

We are everywhere. We see and hear everything. We know who associates with who, who speaks to who; we even know what they have said...

Some of our members act as *orejas,* the 'ears'; they can recognize an enemy by the way he talks. If he speaks against landlords, he is marked; the same if he speaks against the military, or against Yanquis.

Other members act as *ojos,* the 'eyes'; they can tell a subversive by what he does: if he attends a meeting of the peasant cooperative, or is seen speaking to trade union members...

It's the *dedos'* job, once a subversive has been identified, first, to give him a warning — they are the 'fingers' of ORDEN. They may visit him in the middle of the night, or they may pass him a message through one of his children.

But if he doesn't heed the warning and continues his subversive activities, the *dedos* will have to kidnap him. Then we will make an example of him. Every ORDEN member in the district takes part in the lesson: *to indoctrinate the peasants as to the advantages of the democratic system and the disadvantages of the communist system....* This is our purpose. It's usually done with machetes.

Because we're a brotherhood, the blood is on everyone's hands. Your initiation into ORDEN is sealed in blood. Once a member, you belong for life. To try to leave ORDEN would mean death — *Our Fatherland or Death!*

3. A Grudge

One *campesino* said that he could never sleep
for fear that somebody would come in the night
and take him from his house.

Why? Because of two neighbors
in the service of the provincial Army comandante—
both members of the paramilitary ORDEN. Other villagers,
whom these two were known to have grudges against,
had previously disapppeared in the night
only to be discovered later with their throats cut.
And these two men now had a grudge against him...

And one day they *did* come for him;
but he had been warned,
and was in hiding with his family —
except for one son, just a boy,
who they caught and interrogated.

Demanding, "Where is your father?
Tell us where your father is."
they struck his son in the chest
with their rifle butts, again and again:
"Tell us! Tell us where your father is!"

4. The *Guardia Nacional*

We are the National Guard.
Our job is to defend property,
which is sacred.
We don't speak, we act.
We are hard as steel.
We never laugh.
We never crack a smile.
In the civilian's eyes,
we *are* Authority.

We arrest, denounce or capture
anyone who speaks against the landlords —
that's our job.
We torture and kill
not because we like to
but because we must,
to make an example to teach a lesson
about property and authority.

The civilian is a liar,
a thief and a cheat.
He must be dealt with harshly.
Our job is to keep him in line.
The civilian is ignorant;
his mind is poisoned with ideas. Our job
is to teach him what's right.

He is selfish and envious;
the civilian wants and wants
what he can't have:
"Give him a hand," we say,
"and the civilian will take an arm."
To teach him the rules of democracy,
to teach him
to respect private property,
we must be unbending, like steel.

5. The General

*Salvadoran Army General Jose Alberto
   'Chele' Medrano, Speaks:*

In this revolutionary war,
the enemy
comes from our people.
They are traitors to the country.
They don't have the rights of Geneva.
When we find them,
we kill them;

not just the men
who are known subversives,
but the women too,
who are factories
producing more subversives;
and, yes, even the children
who are the future subversives.

Subversive ideas, we say in the Army,
are like seeds growing on a tree
that is shaken by the wind.
The wind causes the seeds to drop. The same wind
carries them to other places
where they fall on fertile soil.
To be rid of subversive ideas
it is necessary
to make the ground sterile.

6. The Ring

In the northern Department of Chalatenango,
a ring of burnt grass and brush was found
where Army troops
had encircled a village with fire
to prevent the inhabitants from escaping.

The bodies of forty-one peasants
were discovered inside the ring.
All had been shot;
many bore gashes and stab wounds
from machetes, bayonets...

7. A Lesson

Campesinos returning
after soldiers had moved on to the next valley
found their villages in ruins:
houses razed to the ground,
clothing ripped and charred,
their possessions strewn about,
every thing of value stolen.
They found that the soldiers had destroyed garden plots;
had burned or carried off food stores;
had shot pigs, chickens, cows, pets...
leaving the carcasses to rot.

While soldiers plundered their hamlet,
campesinos in one valley
hid on the mountainside. They returned later
only to find that relatives and neighbors
had been hacked to death with machetes.
One was found with an arm sliced off,
another was decapitated,
the head lying some distance from the body;
all had been piled in a heap by the soldiers,
and now birds and dogs were feeding on the corpses.

In a different valley, one of the village dogs
trotted out to greet those returning,
carrying a dead infant in its mouth.
On a half-ruined wall, these words were scrawled in chalk:
"This is what happens to those who give aid to subversives."

8. 'Subversive'

> "Soon the Bible and Gospels won't be allowed across the
> borders of El Salvador. We'll get only the bindings, because
> all the pages are 'subversive'." — Rev. Rutilio Grande

A woman testified that soldiers who had taken
her husband and brother away to be shot
threatened to return and kill her also,
saying that she too had been identified as a 'subversive';
and so she fled
to a neighboring village where she had relatives,
although six months pregnant at the time
with her tenth child.

But the soldiers traced her to the house
of the aunt who had taken her in,
and, there, threatened her again. However, the aunt
intervened and stopped the soldiers from killing her
by arguing with them,
insisting that her niece was not a 'subversive,'
convincing the soldiers that they were mistaking
her niece for a different woman
whose husband they had earlier shot.

As soon as the soldiers departed,
the two women ran out,
leaving the chores
and everything in the house as it was—
a wise decision, they realized after:
that evening the soldiers returned,
and when they could not find either woman,
set fire to the aunt's house.

From their hiding place on the mountainside,
the two watched the aunt's house burn to the ground.
As the woman tells it, first the roof fell in,
then, like petals of a flower opening,
the walls collapsed outward
raising a cloud of sparks that lit up the night.

9. Testimony

He wishes to remain anonymous...
a *campesino* from the village of Jicaro,
near Las Minas, Chalatenango Department.

On Tuesday, 13th May,
when government troops descended on his village,
he was preparing a small plot of land for planting corn.
Earlier that morning, a helicopter had passed
several times overhead, surveying the area.
Later, he looked up from his tilling,
to see the helicopter again pass by;
it was then he saw a great number of soldiers, perhaps 900,
converging on Jicaro from three directions:
Las Minas, Llana Grande, and Los Betran,
about 300 coming from each direction:
members of the paramilitary ORDEN, the National Guard,
and regular Army troops.

His neighbor by the name of Soloman Alas was sowing corn.
When the soldiers saw Soloman, they shot and killed him.
Then they killed Jose Melgor and his wife Josefina Guardado;
the brother of Soloman, Salvador Alas;
Jesus Menas and two others. People began fleeing

toward the mountains in the direction of Los Brizuela.
There soldiers entered the house of Adrian Brizuela
and dragged him into the street along with his brother,
     Hermeneguildo.
They shot the one and brutally beat up the other,
leaving Hermeneguildo, bloody and unconscious,
in the street beside the body of Adrian.

There were about 500 in the group from Jicaro fleeing:
men, women, children of all ages, the old, the feeble —
     he among them.
As they went along, peasants from other villages,
of Corral Falco, Las Vueltas, Los Naranjos, joined his group;
for they too had been attacked by the Army and National Guard.

That day,
at the village of El Cacao Concepcion Quetzaltepeque,
soldiers shot dead Jose Bruno Alas, 35 years of age;
Alfonso Mejia, 30; his brother Juan Mejia, 28;
and Jose Israel Orellano, 25. At Los Calles,
they killed an old man, Sebastian Ortiz, 84;
and killed Antonio Palma, 35.

The group arrived at the village of El Potrero
about 2 o'clock in the afternoon;
from there they could see guardsmen atop the hill
        known locally as El Pajal.
They were rolling large rocks down its slopes
trying to crush women and children below.
Several people from among his group were shot there:
Amadeo Mejia, and three children, 11, 7 and 5 years old.

Fearing that soldiers might be waiting in ambush
        in the valley up ahead,
they climbed the mountain, to spend the night.
They were dog-tired, hungry, cold.
A terrible storm lashed them that night;
and because they lacked any shelter on the mountainside,
a three-month-old baby died.

They descended from the mountain at dawn
and continued on in the direction of Los Naranjos.
They were followed closely by soldiers and the National Guard.
A helicopter hovered overhead
and several times swooped down at them.
They passed through the village of Los Amates; there they learned
that two old men had been killed by soldiers that same day:
Carlos Calderon and Juan Lopez.

Arriving at El Zapotel, they heard heavy shooting
from the direction of the Rio Sumpul. They became terrified.
Soldiers were following close behind,
and now soldiers were also up ahead;
and they could see a helicopter in the distance,
hovering over the river.
So they went up into the mountains again,
and stayed there through the night.

At dawn the next day, soldiers were everywhere:
the way to Naranjos was blocked;
there was nowhere to flee.
Most from his group decided to remain in the mountains,
but some — afraid, hungry, thirsty —
broke off from the group to go their own way,
as he did,
back towards El Cacao...

10. The Alternative

Do we want a revolution?
Yes, we want a revolution.
Then even peasants like us could eat meat sometimes —
on feast days or at weddings.

Are we revolutionaries?
Yes, we are.
What we want
is fair payment for the work we do.
If we have to walk 10 kilometers to work in a field
then we want to be given a meal to eat.
And if we cannot return home at night
before the next day's work begins,
then we want to be given a place to sleep.

If we had a revolution,
the hospitals would be open to all the children,
not just children whose parents have ORDEN identity cards.
If your child was sick with diarrhea
you could take him to the pharmacist for medicine
and the pharmacist could sell you the medicine
without fear of getting beaten by the *Guardia.*

What does it mean to be a revolutionary?
It means to fight against soldiers
who kill people who have committed no crime.

At first they bothered only those who spoke up;
they beat them and sometimes tortured them.
Then they began to kill off the leaders. Soon our men
had to go into the hills to sleep at night for safety.
Then they drove whole families from their homes
with threats and beatings.
And if a man went looking for work —
even at the landlord's wages —
he would be shot on sight.

We still went into town to get food and medicine,
but then they began killing any man
who showed his face in the market.

So we sent our sisters and wives;
but they started to kill the women too.
So we sent our children.

An 8-year-old girl went to the market last week
with the few coins her mother had left
to buy an egg for her brother who was sick—
they killed her.

Notes

TREBLINKA:

German Lesson: *Die Verarbeitung,* **Processing** is based principally on Claude Lanzmann's interviews with Franz Suchomel in his Holocaust documentary film *Shoah.*

AUSCHWITZ:

Unforgettable is based on the testimony of Samuel Pisar in "The Death Camps: Liberators and survivors tell of a horrible time."

Unforgettable II, and **First Undress** are based on the testimony of several informants, principally Franz Suchomel and Filip Müller, in Lanzmann's *Shoah.*

Like Butterflies is based on the testimony of Vera Kriegel in "A twin recalls Auschwitz horrors." Added details come from "Victims of Nazi Experiments Recall Their Stories in Israel."

CHALATENANGO:

Based on the testimony of refugees from government mandated terror in El Salvador as documented by the Committees on Foreign Affairs of the U.S. Senate and House of Representatives, among others. Some poems closely follow the testimony of a single individual; others are composites of testimony by two or more persons. Still others are imaginative renderings based upon actual testimony, or they freely combine the actual and imagined.

Prologue: *Abuelito:* A freely imagined rendering of details from various sources which crystallized about an image of the white-haired orphan in "Rising to Rebellion": p.33.

1. *Campesinos:* A composite based on interviews with peasants conducted by Tom Fenton, "Empty Belly Makes Salvadoran Peasant a 'Red'," and on details cited in *El Salvador: The Face of Revolution:* pp.100-102. The italicized sections are a combination of direct quotation and paraphrase.

2. ORDEN: Descriptions of the paramilitary's organizational structure and activities by former members of ORDEN in *El Salvador: The Face of Revolution:* pp.100-101, are here woven together with imaginative details. General Medrano's statement of ORDEN's purpose is from "Behind the Death Squads": p.23.

3. A Grudge: Combines testimony by "Woman No. 1" and "Man No. 2" in *Central America,* 1981: pp.26,27.

4. The *Guardia Nacional:* Based on Manuel Argueta's characterizations of the National Guard in *One Day in a Life.*

5. The General: The first stanza is verbatim a statement by Medrano quoted in "Behind the Death Squads":p.23. The second stanza elaborates upon other statements by Medrano. The third stanza paraphrases a saying attributed to General Martinez, head of state during the 1932 *matanza* (which left an estimated 30,000 peasants dead), a saying which, according to Dunkerly, *The Long War,* enjoys lasting currency within the military.

6. The Ring: Based on a report received by *Socorro Juridico,* the Legal Aid Office of the Salvadoran Archbishopric, summarized in "The Plight of Salvadoran Refugees": p. S13379.

7. A Lesson: Summarizes testimony by all the informants interviewed by Rep. Barbara Mikulski during the House Committee on Foreign Affairs fact-finding visit to refugee camps along the Honduran/Salvadoran border and published in *Central America, 1981:* pp.26-29. Additional details are drawn from "The Battle of Guazapa": p. 47.

8. 'Subversive': Based on the testimony of "Woman No. 4" in *Central America, 1981:* p.28.

9. Testimony: Paraphrases the testimony given by one survivor of the Rio Sumpul massacre as printed in translation in "The Plight of Salvadoran Refugees": S13378.

10. The Alternative: Draws on the comments of a group of peasants hiding in the mountains near Aguilares as recorded by Allman in "Rising to Rebellion":pp. 33- 34.

Sources

Allman, T.D. "Rising to Rebellion," *Harper's* March 1981.

Argueta, Manlio. *One Day in a Life.* Trans. Bill Brow. New York: Random House, 1983.

Armstrong, Robert & Shenk, Janet. *El Salvador, The Face of Revolution.* Boston: South End Press, 1982.

Bikel, Ofra. *Captive in El Salvador* (Frontline #209). Boston: WGBH-TV Transcripts, 1984.

Blundy, David. "Victims of the Massacre that the World Ignored," *Sunday Times of London,* Feb. 22,1981.

Dunkerley, James. *The Long War: Dictatorship & Revolution in El Salvador.* London: Verso Editions, 1983.

Fenton, Tom. "Empty Belly Makes Salvadoran Peasant a 'Red'," *Miami Herald* 27 April 1978.

Kaufman, Jonathan. "The Death Camps: Liberators and survivors tell of a horrible time," *Boston Globe,* April 1, 1985.

Lanzman, Claude. *Shoah,* a Holocaust documentary film.

Nairn, Allen. "Behind the Death Squads," *Progressive* May 1984.

"The Battle of Guazapa," *Newsweek,* April 25, 1983.

U.S. Congress, House of Representatives, Committee on Foreign Affairs. *Central America, 1981: Report of the Committee on Foreign Affairs,* 96th Congress, First Session. Washington: U.S. Government Printing Office, 1981.

U.S. Congress, Senate, Committee on Foreign Affairs. "The Plight of Salvadoran Refugees." *Congressional Record— Senate:* 96th Congress, Second Session, 24 September 1980: S13375-S13379.

"Victims of Nazi Experiments Recall Their Stories in Israel," *New York Times,* February 5, 1985.

Wilkie, Curtis. "A twin recalls Auschwitz horrors," *Boston Globe,* February 5, 1985.